The Cry of the Spirit

The Spirit comes to the aid of our weakness. We do not even know how we ought to pray, but through our inarticulate groans the Spirit himself is pleading for us, and God who searches our inmost being knows what the Spirit means.

Romans 8.26f.

Rex Chapman

The Cry of the Spirit

SCM PRESS LTD

334 00284 2

First published 1974
by SCM Press Ltd
56 Bloomsbury Street London

Printed in Great Britain by
Northumberland Press Ltd
Gateshead

To the parish of St Thomas, Stourbridge

To the congregation of King's College Chapel, University of Aberdeen and

To all who have been part of the eucharistic group which meets in my home

Thanks and peace

Contents

Introduction

If I were asked to write an autobiographical history of my attempts at prayer it would make a haphazard story of fits and starts with long gaps with nothing to report. If you who read this were asked to attempt such an exercise too, for many of you it would probably be the same, though perhaps for a few there might be shorter intervals of nothing. There is an ambiguity in the experience of prayer, and our understanding of it has to embrace the 'nothingness' as well as the 'something'. Thus to begin with biblical material might be to provide a helpful focus.

My only claim for these meditative prayers is that they *are* my own, my own attempt at seeking some measure of growth and development in my understanding and experience of the Christian faith. They are for me the beginnings of a way into prayer. Perhaps they will be of help to others. The meditations in this collection are based on the following New Testament writings – the Acts of the Apostles, the Pauline correspondence, the letter to Hebrews, the short letters of James, Peter, John and Jude, and the Revelation of John. They complete a series of biblically-based prayers begun in *A Kind of Praying* (on the gospels) and continued in *Out of the Whirlwind* (on the Old Testament).

If the reader intends to use these meditations consecutively, I would suggest that he reads the writings on which they are based as a whole, making use of the meditations in so far as they are found helpful in aiding his own reflections and prayers. The reader could also, if he wished, dip into them in connection with Sunday worship as many of them focus on material included in a large number of the passages appointed as readings for the Epistle in the Anglican Lectionary and the Sunday Lectionary of the Joint Liturgical Group.

I would like to thank Miss Irene Thompson for typing the final draft of this book, all those who have been kind enough either to write or to speak to me about my previous meditations, and also my wife and my parents for valuable comments and support during the preparation of these meditations for publication.

University of Aberdeen
September 1973

From Jerusalem to Rome

The Acts of the Apostles provide the source material for the meditations in this opening section. The Acts were written by Luke as a sequel to his gospel to illustrate through selected incidents how Christianity spread from Jerusalem, the centre of the Jewish world, to Rome, the centre of the known Gentile world. Luke unfolds his story to reveal that it is the Spirit of God who is behind the missionary outreach of the church.

The Known and Unknown Lord

Acts 1.1-11; Romans 10.9-21; Philippians 2.9-11

Lord of creation,
Lord of all,
You stand enthroned above the heavens,
Giving courage and strength to your witnesses,
To all who proclaim your Lordship from Jerusalem 'to the ends of the earth'.
Lord of creation,
Lord of all,
You stand enthroned above the heavens,
Giving wisdom and knowledge to those who know you not,
To all within 'the bounds of the inhabited world'.

Bring us together, Lord.
Let the Spirit that guides our mission join with the Spirit that works incognito and unknown in the minds of men,
'That at the name of Jesus every knee shall bow, and every tongue confess "Jesus Christ is Lord" to the glory of God the Father'.

Is Providence so Precise?

Acts 1.15-26; Mark 15.24

Decisions made
At the throw of a dice or the thrust of a pin,
At the toss of a coin or the drawing of lots.
The shirt of Jesus for one man, the trousers for another.
Matthias to join the apostolic club; no vacancy for Joseph Barsabbas.
A chancy decision with the status of providence.
Is providence so precise?
Is it so clearly distinguishable from chance?
Is every little detail so easily planned that we simply sit back and wait for it to be revealed?
Does a prayer over the lottery make all that difference?
Or are we expected on matters of importance to choose and bear the consequences?

Let us work together, Lord.
Increase our sensitivity to your will so that our choices are your choices, and it is not merely left to chance, even a providential chance.

The Spirit of Time Past

Acts 2.1-21; Galatians 5.22-25

Sensation!
Read all about it!
The last days have arrived!

At 9 o'clock this morning, the day of Pentecost, there were some strange meteorological happenings observed in the sky over Jerusalem, which had a bizarre effect on a small group of people from Galilee. With what appeared to be a halo of fire round the heads of each of them they began speaking in a variety of foreign languages. Some of the onlookers thought that they had been drinking, but this seems unlikely so early in the morning. The leader of the group is called Peter and, when interviewed, he said that these events were the direct result of the Spirit of God. He believed that some of our older readers would be having some interesting dreams tonight. Also in the light of information received parents are advised to contact their doctors immediately if they see any unusual behaviour in their sons and daughters. The BBC have indicated that they will keep viewers and listeners informed with up-to-the-minute bulletins of this extraordinary event ...

Here we have the dramatic touch,
But I prefer the more prosaic.
'The fruits of the Spirit are love, joy, peace, patience, kindness, goodness, fidelity, gentleness and self-control.'
The Spirit is the source of life.
Lord, give me life.

Early Enthusiasm

Acts 2.42-47, 4.32-37

It would be easy for a sophisticated century to smile at this story of enthusiasm and naivety.
Once the capital is realized to meet the needs of the needy, it is only a short time before all are needy.

It would be easy for a modern materialistic man to look back in envy at this story of joy in community and freedom from the chains of property.
The early church becomes the ideal church to be born again.

The truth perhaps lies somewhere between the two.

Be with us, Lord.
Here now,
In this place,
At this moment,
In fellowship and joy.

The Threat of Healing

Acts 3.1-4.22

A middle-aged man given new life becomes the centre of controversy.
The leaders must be off their heads.
Haven't I been cured? – I, a cripple from birth, doomed to play the beggar, the Lazarus-role, at the temple gate.
These two, Peter and John, have given me hope for the future, real life for the first time – which is more than religion and the temple have done.
Can't you rejoice with me, you rulers?
How can healing be wrong?
Is the boldness of 'untrained laymen' so threatening to you that you try to muzzle even the Lord?
In the end you can do nothing, but you cause enough suffering on the way.

Lord, give me sense.
Let me share your mind.
Let me evaluate all that I see in terms of your love.
Let me see with your eyes through the mists of prejudice and pride.

For Better, for Worse, for Richer, for Poorer, till Death ...

Acts 5.1-11; Luke 12.10

Now they have done it!
The 'unforgivable sin'.
The sin against the Holy Spirit.
Did the story arise perhaps from linking the sudden death of a couple with their known half-hearted belief in communal living?
We would expect those who shared all to insist on the gravity of keeping something back for oneself.
To loose our hold on things is hard enough at the best of times, but it is well-nigh impossible without the support of all.
So their deaths must be due to their greed.
They have put the Holy Spirit to the test.
No wonder 'great awe fell on the whole church'.
Others would see and learn of the dangers of a bit of private enterprise on the side.
The story perhaps has been touched up in the telling.
I hope so at least, because otherwise it becomes impossible to justify this misuse of apostolic power.
But the point is this:
Not even our innermost secrets are hidden from you, Lord.
I presume on your love when I hold back parts of myself while pretending a total faith.
Work within.
Live within.
Be within.
Turn me inside out towards you.

Gamaliel's Good Sense

Acts 5.13-42

A man of sound common sense.
That's Gamaliel.
It's so simple and obvious, once it's pointed out.
There is no need for all the fuss.
If their message is their own, it will collapse soon enough.
But if it's not, if God is behind it all, no amount of trials and prison sentences will be able to bring it to an end.
So they took his advice, but threw in a flogging to release their own feelings and to show where they thought the source of it lay.

Lord, strengthen those who suffer for their faith.
Would I be strong enough to rejoice in being found worthy to suffer indignity for your sake?
Lord, do not bring me to the test, lest I have to find out.

Let the Gospel be One

Acts 6.1-15

Division within the church from the start.
Was this only the tip of the iceberg? –
A practical matter that concealed beneath it the gulf between two groups of people, Jews from the homeland and Jews who had travelled abroad, with different cultures behind them?
And so an *ad hoc* committee was appointed to sort it all out.

Division within the church from the start.
The Twelve to preach the word, while others wait at table.
The Twelve, Jews from the homeland, whose feet had been washed by the Lord, must get down to prayers and preaching.
Let others see to the widows – widows from the Dispersion.

Division within the church from the start,
Healed by a 'man full of faith and the Spirit',
Who didn't 'neglect the word of God in order to wait at table',
But found himself doing both.

Lord, let whatever insight into the gospel I have flow into prayer, words and action.
Let the gospel be one.

A Martyr's Death or a Murderer's Resurrection?

Acts 6.8-7.1, 7.51-8.1a

A man modelled on the Lord,
Overshadowing the Twelve,
Martyred, like his master, for touching the men of the Council on the raw.
Was his death the beginning of the resurrection of Paul?
Was this the beginning of a chain of events that led to the conversion of this man who watched and approved of the murder?

The future is always unclear.
Consequences are only partly predictable.
All Stephen knew as he died was his Lord.
Strengthen, Lord, the faith of your church, of us, of me.
And usc whatever faith you find to mould the future.

Power in his Hands

Acts 8.9-25

What is the cash value of the Spirit?
A cost benefit analysis of its power makes it a desirable buy,
A bargain at the price!
Power in his hands!
They would have to be insured of course –
They were to be his future livelihood –
And with no excepting clause about acts of God.
For they were to be the very instruments of these acts.

You work through us, Lord.
And how easy it is to claim our glory and our achievements for ourselves.
Work through us only so far as the glory goes to its proper source.

A Eunuch Recharged

Acts 8.26-40

Ethiopia was at the end of the world,
Far removed from the thought-patterns of the Jews.
He is a modern enough man in his failure to understand the prophet.
Yet his sympathies were clear, and he was well on the way to understanding.
The gospel speaks to a man where he is.
There is no need to force the good news down his throat.
Let us be adaptable, Lord.
Let us speak to the point.

The Great Change

Acts 9.1-25; Galatians 1.11-24

Hysterical blindness perhaps.
The ideal excuse for not doing in Damascus what he had set out to do but at the depths of himself was beginning to feel to be wrong.
It gave him a few crucial days to sort himself out,
A few days in which to rethink his faith,
And to come to terms with all that had previously seemed to run counter to his upbringing and all that he had been taught.
What a shock for the orthodox at this conversion of a pillar of the establishment!
It was a lot to live down.
There would be resentment at the change,
And a few seeds of anxiety sown within them about the rightness of their own position.
At least they managed to prick his pride by forcing him to leave Damascus by basket.
But there was trouble in store.
They could be sure of that.
A man hot in his hostilities, with fire in his belly, and boundless energy, he had been turned a hundred and eighty degrees in his tracks.
Now his enthusiasm was directed a different way.
The empire was to become his parish.

It is a great thing, Lord, to be able to bear the pains of such a colossal change.
Commitment is costly.
Give me commitment.

A Little Man among the Great

Acts 9.10-17

You must have been very convincing, Lord.
You would have had to pull out all the stops to allay his anxieties,
To make him sure that he wasn't just deluding himself, giving way to wishful thinking.
He was taking his life into his hands.
This venture of his gives him a place among the great men of faith.
A little man among the great.
A more realistic model of faith for most of us, Lord.
The Lord said: Go at once ... so Ananias went.
Strengthen my faith.

Circumcision: To Be or Not To Be

Acts 10.1-11.4, 11.18, 15.1-35; Galatians 3.26-29, 5.6

It was inevitable, I suppose,
Inevitable that it would cause a stir among the Jewish Christians back at home.
Baptism for the uncircumcised.
It meant enlarging their concept of God.
Cornelius was a religious man, it is true, and 'gave generously to help the Jewish people'.
But if he were baptized,
Where would it end?
The new ideas are already spreading like wildfire.
They would be baptizing the Emperor next!

The pressures to exclude always seem stronger than those to welcome in.
The rules, your rules, Lord, as we once saw them, are down in black and white and we intend to stick to them through thick and thin.
It always takes us a little while to catch up with the activity of your Spirit, leading us to a deepening awareness of your love.
We come running along behind and sometimes graciously, sometimes not, we agree to bring our thinking into line with yours.
If you're lucky we give 'praise to God and say, "this means that God has granted life-giving repentance to the Gentiles also" '.
If you are not so lucky we fossilize a new insight with yet more black and white canons and say, 'it is the decision of the Holy Spirit, and *our* decision, to lay no further burden upon you *beyond these essentials.*'

Shake your church wide open, Lord.
Give guidance in the difficulties of deciding your will in the practical matters that confront us.
Bring us into union with you.
Give us 'the only thing that matters, faith active in love'.

A Messenger of Freedom

Acts 12.1-17; Daniel 3.28

A very practical angel, Lord.
'Do up your belt and put your shoes on.'
A guardian angel with a message from the Lord.
You are the source of freedom from the chains that ensnare a man's life.
Bring freedom.

The Gods are Among Us

Acts 14.8-20

The gods are among us,
Working their wonders.
Come and make sacrifice.
Men become gods when some power they have is seen to prevail upon us,
When we can worship them for their wisdom and strength.

The boy was impressed with the knowledge and skill of a teacher.
He built him up in his mind to gigantic proportions,
And had him well on the way to Olympus,
Until years later the image was shattered.
The god had become man.

The men of Lystra were soon persuaded to demythologize their gods,
And they turned against them when the illusions were broken.

We are always on the look out, Lord, for a god among us,
For a Führer to lead us to heaven.
Then we only need to follow.
You are our God, Lord, and you lead from within.
Turn us from these follies to your own living self.

Profit, Prison and Forgiveness

Acts 16.16-39

The profit motive is all that counts.
It demands sacrifices.
It devours lives.
It runs wild when its altar is bare.
So the two of them are thrown into gaol for giving a girl freedom.
But it's so patently unjust that when morning comes they stand fast and wait for the over-officious magistrates to come in person to escort them out.
It's enough to try to shame them into being less overbearing in the future.
For the rest forgiveness.
No compensation is asked.

One, Two, Three, Four, Who Are We For? D-I-A-N-A

Acts 19.23-34

I don't know what they were worrying about.
Image-makers are versatile enough.
It's just a matter of changing the images.
One day Diana, the next day a cross, or a plastic saint.
In all sizes,
For all pockets,
You name it, we stock it.
If the demand weren't there at first, I am sure that they would be able to create it.
A plaque of Paul for hanging on your wall,
Made from genuine Ephesian silver!
Change Diana's name to Mary and they wouldn't even have obsolete stock on their hands.
Their business acumen was slipping!
Here was a new market in the making.

Lord,
Break the images.
Make them only windows on to your reality.

Tender Scruples

Acts 21.18-26; Romans 8.1-2, 15.1-2

The word was abroad that Paul was turning his back on the religion of his people in favour of the Gentiles.
So he agrees to go through the motions of purification.
Partly conviction, perhaps, partly convenience.
He was a Jew and the ritual would be part of his nature.
Yet he knew it to have been totally transformed,
It no longer mattered.
'The life-giving law of the Spirit has set you free from the law of sin and death.'
So he undertakes it for the gospel's sake, to avoid scandal and to make it easier for Jewish Christians to bear the breaking of barriers.

Give patience, Lord,
Patience in the face of seeming irrelevancies, tender scruples,
Patience so long as the scruples aren't to be imposed on us all.

An Unholy Alliance

Acts 22.30-23.15

Paul was no fool.
Divide the Council and they will show themselves for what they are –
Angry men with axes to grind,
An unholy alliance revealed.
No pretence of justice.
Only a blinkered crowd seeing a bit of the truth, and denying a whole lot more.
They are likely to tear themselves apart as much as Paul.
And they will probably hate him the more for revealing their dissensions.
Now the cry is murder.

A cautionary tale, Lord.
Give prudence when we come to deny another man's faith.
All that we can really affirm is what we ourselves know from experience to be true.

The Roman Jew

Acts 24.1-26.32

An articulate man among articulate men,
With all his wits about him for his defence.
Now he was on his way to Rome with no charges against him that could possibly stick.
He departs as a criminal but it is his accusers who are on trial.
I doubt if this is how he would have wished to visit Rome.
But to Rome he went,
The symbolic messenger of the Spirit,
The link between Palestine and Rome, the past and the future,
A Roman Jew.

Your Spirit, Lord, inspires men and works your will within them.
Dare I ask you to work within me,
Not knowing in advance the implications?
Dare I?

The End of One Road, the Beginning of the Next

Acts 28.16-31

At the heart of empire,
The good news has arrived.
Much has happened since those early days in Jerusalem many years ago.
Would Paul look back over his life and sense the achievement?
The Jewish sect was on its way to becoming an international religion.
Would he look back and feel disappointment too?
His own people 'hear and hear, but never understand'.
They are the elect, the ones chosen from among the rest, with the truth, the whole truth, enshrined in their Law.
What further need is there for 'good news'?
The ones who listen are the ones who are far from satisfied with themselves.

Lord, achievements and disappointments are interwoven throughout life.
Build on the one,
And let the other be the spur to deeper faith in your power.

From Tarsus with Love

On any reckoning Paul of Tarsus was one of the great men of history. We may not always agree with him. We may find some of his theological ideas difficult to grasp. But it is undeniable that he played a part of profound significance in developing the church's understanding of itself and in enabling it to grow from a sect within Judaism to a religious force that was eventually to grip the Gentile world.

In the following pages we base our reflections on passages from his letters. There are thirteen letters from that to the Romans to the short note to Philemon ascribed to St Paul in the New Testament, though there is considerable doubt as to whether in fact they are all genuine. (The fourteenth letter, to the Hebrews, is generally no longer regarded as Pauline.) For further information on this one of the books mentioned in the appendix can be consulted. Here our concern is with the content of the letters rather than the question of authorship. We are concerned to let the witness of the early church inform our thoughts and prayers, and if that witness is not only that of Paul but also of other, now anonymous, Christians, then this is gain. The more witnesses there are to the faith of these early days the more comprehensive our understanding might be. The letters to the Romans, Corinthians and Galatians are generally acknowledged as having been written by Paul and those to the Philippians, Colossians, Thessalonians and Philemon might well have been also. If this is so, they would have been written between the early fifties and early sixties AD. About the remaining letters (to the Ephesians, Timothy and Titus) there is greater uncertainty. If they were not written by Paul, then they belong to the period succeeding the sixties up to the turn of the century.

Justice and Love are One

Romans 1.16-17, 3.21-26

The sinner stands judged –
Judged worthy of love.
Justice and love are one.
They have to be one.
For if the justice of God should demand that the sinner be condemned, then the forgiveness of love is unjust.

Lord, you forgive.
You justify.
You liberate.
You die to demonstrate the depth of your justice and your love.
Strengthen the faith that alone makes this effective for a man,
Effective for 'all, without distinction; for all alike have sinned',
Effective even for me.

Faith is the Key

Romans 4.1-3, 13-25

Our father Abraham, the archetypal Jew, conferring privilege on his physical descendants alone who obey the Law.
Our father Abraham, the typical man of faith, the father of all who share his faith in 'the God who makes the dead live'.
Two interpretations of succession.
Our mother church linked through history by hands on heads alone.
Our mother church, the body of faith in 'the God who raised Jesus our Lord from the dead'.

Faith is the key, Lord.
Give us faith.

The Threefold Way

Romans 5.1-2, 8.24; Philippians 2.12; Hebrews 13.8

Past.
Present.
And future.
The threefold way in the workings of God.
The action is over, but still it continues and is yet to come.
'We *have been* justified and saved',
'Though only in *hope*' – 'the hope of the divine splendour that *is to be* ours'.
'Let us *continue* at peace with God . . . in the sphere of God's grace, where *we now stand*', and '*work out our own salvation* in fear and trembling'.

You have acted in Christ, Lord, and acquitted the world, revealing the extent of your love.
You have acted in Christ and said the last word, revealing yourself as you are.
And now it is our turn to answer that word, revealing the extent of our love.
Now it is our turn to answer that word, revealing ourselves as we are.
And then we'll be one, with our hopes fulfilled, for your splendour will have been shared.
Then we'll be one and the world will be free, and time will be lost in your love.

Lord of time and eternity,
Lord of then and now and what is to be,
Draw us along your threefold way.

Suffering and Hope

Romans 5.3-5, 8.18-25

Here is an attempt to gain an understanding of suffering.
'Let us even exult in our present sufferings, because we know that suffering trains us to endure.'
It does not convince.
Suffering is evil.
This has to be said.
However great a man's courage and endurance,
However strong his faith through the trials of persecution,
However much his character and life are strengthened through the testing of pain,
Suffering remains suffering, and it is a summons to us to co-operate in effecting release.
And this you urge us to do, Lord, in the hope that 'the universe itself is to be freed from the shackles of mortality and enter upon the liberty and splendour of the children of God'.
Suffering is evil, but it is not the last word.
Relieve suffering, Lord.
Use us to relieve it.
And hasten the day when 'our whole bodies are set free'.

The Proof of Love

Romans 5.6-11, 8.31-39

I am what I am.
And I am happy as I am.
It is a temptation to say it, Lord,
To say the word of acceptance of myself –
An acceptance based on your acceptance of all men.
For 'there is nothing in all creation that can separate us' from your love.
'Christ died for us while we were yet sinners.'
It is a temptation to say it and stay as I am if I have nothing to lose,
For your love is sure, and we are 'saved from final retribution'.

I am what I am.
I only say it when I stand convicted of failure and sin.
And I say it then as much in reassurance that even as I am you are on my side and pronounce acquittal.
Make me more than I am.
It is impossible to remain the same yesterday, today and for ever in the face of suffering love and sacrificial death.
For the cross is more potent and positive for personal change than any fear of final judgment.
It is the proof of your love.
Make me more than I am.
Let your acceptance and forgiveness and love revolutionize my life.
Let the cost of your death be the cost of my discipleship.

The Ambivalence of Law

Romans 7.7-8.11

The ambivalence of law.
It is 'holy and just and good' for it reveals the seductions of sin.
It points to the will of God, but has no power in itself to raise a man from the lower levels of his existence, the dark reaches of those inner compulsions that act like gravity to hold him down.
'Instead of doing the good things I want to do, I carry out the sinful things I do not want.'
Here is the ambivalence of all rules.
They give guidance but no hope to the man who fails them.
They point the way but have no power within themselves to help us on that way.

Lord, yours is the way.
You are the way,
Releasing within us the power of your Spirit.
For there is hope for the man who knows forgiveness.
There is hope when the sins of the past are expunged.
The tensions are still there.
The problems remain.
But you have declared yourself for man,
Revealing the way and being that way.
The direction is now one of hope.

The Cry of the Spirit

Romans 8.14-17, 26-27; Galatians 4.6-7; Mark 14.32-36

'Abba! Father!'
The essence of prayer.
Words of feeling, words of the Spirit,
Words of awareness of the love and reliability of God.
You are said to utter the words, Lord, on the night before your death.
No ecstatic shoutings here.
But a strengthening of courage to face the future flowing from the knowledge of the nearness and graciousness of God.
You work in the depths of our inmost being.
Your Spirit binds us both together as you speak through 'our inarticulate groans' of acknowledgment.
Pray within us as we pray ourselves.
For we are to be sharers in suffering and splendour.

Sequence of Salvation

Romans 8.29-30, 9.18-23, 11.32-36; 1 Corinthians 12.3; 2 Thessalonians 2.13-14

Known.
Fore-ordained.
Called.
And justified.
The sequence of salvation, starting from the Lord.
If God is sovereign, choosing whom he wills, the men of faith who respond share 'the wealth of his splendour' as 'vessels of mercy'.
Lord, I respond as best I can.

Known.
Fore-ordained.
Called.
And condemned.
The route of retribution, regulated by the Lord.
If God is sovereign, choosing whom he wills, those who exhibit little sign of faith, though 'tolerated very patiently', become 'vessels of retribution due for destruction'.
And his own disobedient people fit the bill.

But the case is overstated if taken to its logical conclusion.
That the initiative is the Lord's is a fact of experience.
That many fail to respond is a fact of life, but to apportion the responsibility is a hazardous affair.
You are free and we are free, and our freedoms overlap.
You freely call and we freely answer, one way or the other.
When that answer is 'yes', the man who makes it knows that you have directed him to his decision.
But when that answer is 'no', the man who makes it could hardly say the same.
Paul too in the end steps back from the brink.
For 'God's purpose was to show mercy to all mankind'.
Let all be part of the sequence of salvation.

Conscience

Romans 9.1, 12.1-2, 13.5; 1 Corinthians 8.7; 1 Timothy 4.1-2; 1 Peter 2.19

Conscience assures a man that he tells the truth.
Its demands are insistent that it should be obeyed,
For it is the voice of God that speaks within him.
But the voice may be weak,
Or totally deformed, 'branded with the devil's sign'.

Conscience is the belief by which a man acts and speaks and decides.
But it is also a control with guilt as its tool,
It is determined and formed by all a man does,
By the circumstances of his life and the influence of others.
You speak through a man's conscience, Lord, and seek to be identified with the voice within.
But you are not always that voice.
The internal demands need to be checked.

Two people come to mind:
The girl was guilt-ridden and enslaved by a conscience that allowed no freedom of choice.
The man had a conscience so well controlled that it almost merged with all his desires.

Speak with strength, Lord.
Burst through a conscience compounded of much that puts a barrier between us.

Let me discern your will.
Let my mind be remade and my whole nature be transformed.
Let me educate and form my conscience as I offer myself to you.
Illuminate it with your Spirit.
Be the light within.

A Collection of Gifts

Romans 12.3-8; 1 Corinthians 12.4-20

An ebullient man with bounce and panache, speaking of his Lord with abandon and ease.
An eloquent man of sophistication and precision measuring his words with care and delight.
A lonely man without confidence and seemingly cynical.
An intellectual man in the clouds making great demands of his hearers.
A man with a smile and a gospel to sell.
An organization man with his files in his head.
A boring man who cannot take a hint.
A warm-hearted man, constantly exploited, constantly giving.
An odd man to stare at and never understand.
An anxious man full of guilt and driving himself hard.
A man to admire with joy and respect.
All men in the body, the body of Christ.
For 'there are many different organs, but the body is one'.
It has to be your Spirit, Lord, working through all.
Nothing else could possibly join us in one.

The System

Romans 13.1-7; 1 Peter 2.13-15; Mark 12.17

Them and us.
The system against freedom?
Law and order or direct action?
No hedging of bets for Paul.
'The authorities ... are God's agents of punishment, for retribution on the offender'.
He of course had received sanctuary from the state, and protection from the hostility of his own people.
He had made much of his Roman citizenship.
And it was only later that Rome roused herself against the church.
Knowing this, would he still have written as he did?
It is dangerous doctrine, that 'existing authorities are instituted by God'.
Sometimes they are and become 'God's agents working for good'.
When they work for reconciliation and love, unity and peace.
But when they strive to separate and enslave, to crush and destroy, to terrify and spread hate, are we not to say that roles become reversed and 'rebels against authority' might well be the ones who are the agents of the Lord?
Obedience is a virtue only when that which is to be obeyed is worth obeying.
Caesar stands second to God.

Lord, let us create society.
Let us 'build the earth'.
Let your kingdom come, your will be done on earth.

The Hope that was Then is the Hope that is Now

Romans 15.4-13; Hebrews 1.1-4

'All the ancient scriptures were written for our own understanding, in order that through the encouragement they give us we may maintain our hope with fortitude.'
The ancient scriptures and hope.
The light at the end of the tunnel.
A thousand years and more of history leading to the Christ.
Here is the justification for the days of the old times.
For the Christ belongs there long before his birth.
'The effulgence of God's splendour',
'The stamp of his being',
'Sustaining the universe by the word of his power'.
The hope once partly seen is now more clearly seen.
The hope that was then is the hope that is now.

Lord of optimism and purpose,
Lord of the hope that runs through history,
We sing praise to your name
And on you we set our sights.

‘From Each according to his Means, To Each ...’

Romans 15.25-27; 2 Corinthians 8.1-9

The proof of the pudding is in the eating.
The spiritual and material are linked.
For ‘the Word was made flesh’,
The rich became poor to make all men rich.
The good news impinges on life at its most material level.
‘From each according to his means, to each according to his need.’
Lord, the gospel takes root in a variety of places.
Let it take root in me.

'I am Christ's'

1 Corinthians 1.4-18, 3.1-11, 3.21-23

'In them the evidence for the truth of Christ has found confirmation',
For they lacked 'no single gift', but were to be kept 'firm to the end, without reproach on the Day of the Lord'.
Among them too evidence of a different kind has found confirmation, evidence for the disunity of the church.
Paul, Apollos, Cephas and Christ – names to be conjured with,
Names to add a touch of respectability to their divisions,
Names they were proud to attach to their groups,
Names of the famous to be grabbed for themselves.
Not even these divisions could abrogate their call, for they were called by God and 'God keeps faith'.
But disunity and Christ are contradictory terms.
For where there are divisions, where is the church?

Heal, Lord,
Reconcile.
Let us not build on this or that understanding of the faith, on this or that detail of truth.
Let us build on Christ.

The Power of God and the Wisdom of God

1 Corinthians 1.18-25; Luke 23.32-34; John 19.30

Jews call for miracles
Give us a sign,
Proof of your power.
Come down from the cross.
Let us see you act in the usual way.
Stick to the divine conventions, if you please.
We have got our picture of you clear in our minds.
The rules of the god-game are fixed.
Don't start changing them now.
You don't expect us to believe, do you, without some proof that will be acceptable to us?
We know the sort of God we want – the God of power who will pulverize all that stands in our way.
Be my God, God, the God *I* want.

Greeks look for wisdom
This Jew is letting his emotions run away with him.
Wisdom is the key that will unlock the doors of the universe.
It is the wisdom of the wise that works wonders.
Intellect is the source of all that advances the human lot.
Reason is power.
Argue your case with us, God, and we will see what we think.
If you are persuasive enough, we will believe.
If you can convince us by the strength of your arguments, we might even agree to debate on your side.
Be my sort of God, God, the God *I* want.

Christ nailed to the cross ... is the power of God and the wisdom of God
It is hard, Lord, to accept you on your own terms.
I sometimes wish that faith were the door to privilege,
The privilege of being able to call on your power to carry out my own will.

But your power is the power of love that shrieks out from the cross
– 'forgive them for they know not what they do'.

It is hard to accept you on your own terms.
The 'wisdom of the wise' is not foolish in itself.
It is the result of a man's questionings and gropings after the truth,
A try for the answers that lie hidden to the gaze.
I sometimes wish that faith were the door to privilege,
The privilege of being able to know the secret of the world.
But reason has its limits.
It is only half of a man.
Your wisdom is the wisdom of love that completes your purpose –
'it is accomplished!'

Share with me, Lord, the power and wisdom of your love.

The Inside of a Man

1 Corinthians 1.26-2.5

What goes on inside a man?
Paul does not strike me as 'low and contemptible, a mere nothing'.
He was an educated Pharisee, with personality and drive,
A leader among men.
But 'I came before you weak, as I then was, nervous and shaking with fear.'
Now, later, his confidence has returned.
And the object of his pride has changed.
Human pride is broken in the presence of God.
It has to be broken before a person can realign himself to be a man.
Then he can be proud, 'proud of the Lord', for it is the Lord who has come within him.

Break false pride, Lord, the pride that takes credit for all that is good and fine within,
But does so at the expense of a total view of all that is within.
Set me free from reliance on the persuasive voice that bolsters the ego and builds me up large.
Set me free to rely upon you.

The Temple of God

1 Corinthians 3.16-17; 1 Peter 2.4-5; Matthew 27.50-51; Psalm 24

The place of meeting.
The scene of worship.
The focus for the presence of God.
The foundations are solid on the rock of Sion.
The holy of holies is in the holiest place in the holy city.
'Who may go up the mountain of the Lord?
And who may stand in his holy place?'

But the curtain of the temple is torn apart.
The walls have burst asunder.
And you are free and uncontrolled, Lord.
Free to create within your people all that temple stood for.
The holiest of holies is now within man.
And the foundations are based in community.
Here now is the place of meeting,
The scene of worship,
The focus of the presence of God.
'Lift up your heads, you gates,
Lift yourselves up, you everlasting doors,
That the king of glory may come in.'

Trustworthiness Judged

1 Corinthians 4

Who can judge whether a man has shown himself trustworthy when so much of the relevant evidence is unknown?
Can others ever know the inner motives of another man's life?
Can the man himself accurately assess the experiences of conscience?
For a clear conscience may be an uneducated conscience uncontrolled by the mind of Christ.
And a guilty conscience may be an overscrupulous conscience warped by influences from without.
Judgments are made but they have to be provisional.
But they do have to be made and Paul freely makes them.
'There are certain persons who are filled with self-importance because they think I am not coming to Corinth.'
While Timothy is a 'most trustworthy Christian who will remind you of the way of life in Christ'.
Yet the point of judging is not to condemn nor to shame, but to change and 'to bring you to reason'.
You alone are the ultimate judge, Lord.
Keep guard over our thoughts and our tongues.

The Evil-Doers

1 Corinthians 5; Mark 1.14-15

One out, all out.
If the evil-doers are to be rooted out, there will be nobody left.
Paul no doubt had in mind open causes of scandal that were likely to bring the church into disrepute,
And perhaps believed that a man 'consigned to Satan' with his sin punished would then be qualified to rise in the spirit on the Day of the Lord.
But the question is:
Where is the line to be drawn?
The atmosphere can be poisoned just as easily by secret scandal that remains unseen.
Perhaps repentance is the clue.
The church is as full of sinners as the world,
But sinners aware of their sin and seeking forgiveness.
The time has come;
The Kingdom of God is upon us.
Lord, I repent.
Help me to believe the gospel,
And to put it into effect.

Conditioned Remarks

1 Corinthians 7; Ephesians 5.21-33

O Lord!
Here we go!
Culturally conditioned remarks turned into the word of God.
But it is by no means as bad as a first careless reading might suggest.
There is much about marriage that is right and good.
And would he have written like this had he known the publicity his letters would eventually get?
'The time we live in will not last long.'
The End was near.
'The whole frame of this world is passing away.'
He was wrong of course and the world goes on.
These remarks lose much of their relevance, thank God,
And stand as a constant reminder of the perils of extending an insight beyond the circumstances from which it grew.
The word of the Lord speaks through men of this time and of that place,
And inevitably belongs to a certain culture and a certain society.
Let us not judge Paul too harshly.
Nor let us swallow his line without thinking.
Let us enable the word of the Lord to speak clearly and with relevance to now.

'All Things to All Men'

1 Corinthians 9.19-27

The fundamentals are few.
The essential matters for the guidance of one's life.
The basic absolutes for which a man might even die.
'Hold to Christ, and for the rest be totally uncommitted.'

But then there are those who seem to make mountains out of molehills,
Who surround their lives with a network of rules,
And live like a spider at the centre of a web that ensnares the unwary.
Strict training is required here, Lord.
'To become weak, to win the weak.'
Strict training to see the wood for the trees.
And the strictest of training in humility and patience.
For otherwise we think ourselves strong
And the arrogance of pride drops like a blanket on the small flames of your Spirit within.

Stay with us, Lord, so that we do not find ourselves rejected.

‘A Memorial of Me’

1 Corinthians 10.16-17, 11.23-28

He lay in bed for three years before he finally died.
Although he could not move very much,
He looked the same,
And he was recognized and cared for by those who were near him.
But to all intents and purposes his mind had been wiped clean by a stroke.
He remembered nothing.
He recognized nobody.
He was on his own.

‘Do this as a memorial of me.’
The church is on its own,
Paralysed and inert,
Unless it shares in its common memory of Christ.
To remember a man is to bring that man into the present.
It is to recall him from the past so that his presence in the mind at least has influence now.
It is to invoke a happening of then to affect a happening now.
It is to remind oneself of an event that once had power so that its power can be made effective again.
To remember in action the Christ broken and killed is ‘to proclaim the death of the Lord’ to all who care to listen.

Lord, I remember;
Enable me to remember.
Lord, we remember;
Let us share the memory as one.

Love and Crosses

1 Corinthians 13; Romans 13.8-10; 1 John 4.7-12

A lesson on love and profoundly moving.
'There is nothing that love cannot face.'
Though as it stands more needs to be said.
A man loves a friend.
A husband loves his wife.
A father loves his child.
There is much in common but the emotional overtones are very different.
Love is a word that covers a multitude of things, from lying in a haystack to dying on a cross.
Paul's lesson on love has cross as commentary.
Faith falls away with the wholeness of knowledge.
And hope has its end in the fulfilment of creation.
But love lasts for ever because God is love,
And 'God dwells in us if we love one another' –
With the suffering love that we see on the cross.

Body Building

1 Corinthians 14.26, 15.35-36; Ephesians 4.11-12, 16

The church was built by the gifts of its members and is a glorious expression of praise.
But now it is old and the thermometer stands beside it, declaring its temperature to the world.
With ten thousand pounds given and ten thousand to go, the ailing building desperately clings to life.
But can the seed produce life unless it has first died?

Building the church is building the body and the body can thrive without buildings.
Perhaps some are needed and need to be saved, but many are not and ought not to be saved.
But this is a secondary matter, Lord.
Use our talents, our energies, our gifts 'to equip your people for work in your service'.
Let us build the body of Christ.

A Creed in the Making

1 Corinthians 15.1-11

Dead.
Risen.
Experienced.
A sermon in shorthand.
A summary of the gospel.
A signpost to faith.
A creed in the making.
'This is what we all proclaim and this is what you believed.'
'Facts imparted to me and handed on to you.'
An act of God in the lives of men.
But an ongoing act that takes them in its grip,
Turning disciples into apostles.

The creeds slip out, Lord, every day.
Let them inspire to action.
Let the deeds they bear witness to take root in your disciples now.
Make us apostles.

'Even to Me'

1 Corinthians 15.3-11, 20; Acts 9.1-19; Galatians 1.1

The beginning of it all for Paul.
The experience of grace.
An experience to colour and mould the meaning of his faith.
An experience to determine the key to his outlook on life.
'By God's grace I am what I am.'
This belief was unshakeable.
He could not deny it without denying a piece of his own personal past.
He could not deny it without denying a piece of his own personal present.
'In my labours I have outdone them all – not I, indeed, but the grace of God working with me.'
In the beginning, God.
In the middle, God.
And in the end, God.
For 'the truth is, Christ was raised to life as the first fruits of the harvest of the dead.'

Let me look, Lord, to your action within me.
Let me see your work and believe.
'Appear even to me.'

Resurrection Hope

1 Corinthians 15.12-58

Here is a mixture of tremendous hope and one man's way of interpreting that hope.
Resurrection is miracle
And the miraculous is under attack.
Paul leaps to its defence.
It is an important matter and much is at stake.
'Why do we face these dangers hour by hour? ... If the dead are never raised to life, "let us eat and drink, for tomorrow we die".'
This argument does not work.
The Christian way is the human way to be followed come what may.
Once it becomes an enterprise to be embarked upon for the rewards of risen life, our way is lost.
Strengthen me to follow, Lord, whether or not there is to be 'life after death' for me.

But I cannot finish here.
More needs to be said.
For 'in Christ *all* will be brought to life'.
Now 'O Death, where is your victory? O Death, where is your sting?'
The future is unclear and unknown, but however slight my experience of you, Lord, it suggests that a future there must be.
To live in Christ is to live in you, and to live in you is eternal life, now as much as later.
Hope and joy and love are lasting values.
You subject all things to yourself.
You 'will be all in all',
And in you nothing can be lost.

What is it that I Reflect?

2 Corinthians 3.6-18, 4.5-7; Exodus 34.29-35

He was an influence for good.
He had a charisma and flair, and an ability to make a man feel at home.
He was an ordinary enough person in many ways, but reliable and strong in the Spirit.
He reflected something that it is hard to pin down, but something that made him the sort of person it was good to be with.
'Because for us there is no veil over the face, we all reflect as in a mirror the splendour of the Lord.'
This is a thought that makes sense when applied to him, but a terrifying thought when applied to ourselves.
We know ourselves too well.
The mirror is cracked, the image distorted.
'We are no better than pots of earthenware to contain this treasure.'
Forgive us, Lord,
And transfigure us into your likeness.
This you can do, for 'such is the influence of the Lord who is Spirit'.
Transfigure us and cause your light to shine within us.

A New World of Unknown Men

2 Corinthians 5.14-17, 6.3-10

The startling change.
'Penniless, we own the world,'
The 'new world' of 'unknown men'.
The value system of society has been overthrown.
'Worldly standards have ceased to count.'
The myth of success and failure is broken on a cross.
For the supreme failure is the supreme success.
The man who died with a mission in ruins has become the man who lives as the symbol of life.
The man who died feeling forsaken by his God has become the man who lives at the centre of God.
The man who lost everything has become the man who gained all.
The myth is broken, and man is free.

It is an ambiguous victory for me, Lord.
When failure is real and life at a low ebb, the victory is glorious and gives me strength.
But when success and fame fall my way, I am eager to latch on to them like a leech and feed on their strength.
But it is a precarious strength that knows nothing of failure and has nothing to give when its demands are not met.
The myth of success and failure is broken on a cross.
Strengthen me, Lord, to enable it to be broken in me.
Encourage me to know in experience that
'Dying we live.'

In Christ

2 Corinthians 5.18-21; 1 Corinthians 15.22; Colossians 1.19-20, 2.9

The meeting of Maker and Man.
The centre of it all.
The point of creation.
The Christ.
For God was in Christ.
And man is in Christ.
And all things come to completion in Christ.

Adam was man but Adam is dead.
Christ is the new man and Christ is alive.

Come, Lord, hold our misdeeds against us no more.
Unite us with Christ for Christ is yourself.
Come, Lord, entrust us with the message of reconciliation.
Unite us with Christ for Christ is mankind.
We too are 'one with the sinfulness of men'.
Come, Lord, make us one with the goodness of yourself.
Let us join and co-operate in remaking man.
For you are God and you are man and never the twain shall split.

The Effect of Censure

2 Corinthians 7.8-13; 1 Peter 2.19-25

The effect of censure is uncertain.
A vote of censure was passed, Lord, on your own view of yourself, as you were led away to the cross.
A lesser god might have reacted in anger against the arrogance of the accusation and destroyed all in his path.
A frail god might have climbed back into his shell broken and downhearted, all love inhibited.
A paranoid god might have seen it all as an atheistic plot against his plans, with a suspicious eye seeing hostility in every corner.
But your model is not man and you bore your hurt in your own way.
'When he was abused he did not retort with abuse, when he suffered he uttered no threats.'
And you, Lord, had 'committed no sin'.

For the Corinthians it was different for they had 'to clear themselves of blame'.
But 'by your wounds we have been healed'.
They 'were straying like sheep, but have now turned towards the Shepherd and Guardian of their souls'.

Enable us to cope with censure, Lord,
To react as you react.

Obliged to Boast?

2 Corinthians 11.16-12.11, 3.4-6; Mark 14.60-61

I feel for you, Paul.
What does a man do if his work is attacked,
Especially if the attack is totally unfounded,
And especially too if the man is miles away from the scene of the charge and has to respond by letter?
The temptation to justify oneself is very great.
The temptation to spread it on thick or explode in anger takes a firm hold within.
You hold back your anger, Paul, except for some sarcasm – 'how gladly you bear with fools being yourselves so wise!'
But you laid your achievements down the line, and yet felt foolish doing it – 'my credentials should have come from you Corinthians'.
Perhaps, like me, you remember the silence of that man from Nazareth when on trial for his life and wish you had the strength to follow.
And yet should I not speak for their sake and for the sake of the church?
It is a difficult dilemma.
'I am obliged to boast. It does no good; but I shall go on ...'
It does no good, but still we do it.

Lord, let me take your answer to Paul as an answer to myself.
'My grace is all you need',
For 'such qualification as we have comes from you'.

The Power of Powerlessness

Ephesians 1.15-23; 2 Corinthians 12.9-10

A conception on the grand scale, Lord.
'How vast the resources of his power!'
I like the idea of the power, but I am not so keen about the way in which it is seen.
For it is a power than can be realized only when it is discarded,
A power that exerts its authority for all time in and through a cross,
A power that is found in powerlessness.

And what an exalted picture of the church! –
Holding within it 'the fullness of him who himself receives the entire fullness of God'.
A picture that panders to all the triumphalist tendencies that lurk within us.
But here is the rub:
This fullness of power within the church that subjects all things to itself is the power of suffering and service.
Here is 'the glory of Christ in the church'.

Lord, empty our pretensions to grandeur of all their meaning,
Let us laugh them out of their hold upon us.
What power you share with us comes only through our powerlessness,
For 'power comes to its full strength in weakness'.

The Initiative is Yours

Ephesians 2.1-10; Galatians 2.20

I am thankful that you take the initiative, Lord.
You lead,
You guide.
You go before us,
Bringing us in spite of ourselves to life in you.
You set the spark alight and nurture the flame,
You leave us with no cause for boasting of our feats,
For whatever good we do is the work of your Spirit within us.
This is humbling, Lord,
But consoling too.
For you ask of me nothing that I cannot in some small measure give.
You ask for my faith so that you can work your will within.
'Lord, I believe; help my unbelief.'

There are Walls and Walls

Ephesians 2.13-22, 4.1-6

'In his own body he has broken down the enmity which stood like a dividing wall between Gentiles and Jews.'
The dividing wall is broken,
The dividing wall of feelings and thoughts, of opinions and plans,
The wall of insecurity and prejudice,
The wall that defends us from the contamination that comes from without,
The one we have so laboriously built to hide our anxieties or protect our privilege.
The wall is breached, but it is not yet down.
And we are working like slaves to man the defences and shore up the stones.

The wall that matters, Lord, is that of which you are the foundation,
The wall of the 'spiritual dwelling' into which you are building mankind.
Come, Lord.
Be the bond who binds us together,
Bringing peace to all on the other sides of the walls which divide,
'Peace to those far off, and peace to those who are near.'
You are our solidarity, our hope for community, the 'one Lord who is over all and through all and in all',
Creating out of discord a 'single new humanity' in yourself.
And enable us too to make fast that unity which you give.

It's as Broad as it's Long

Ephesians 3.14-21; Psalm 139.1-12

O ye metaphors and myths,
O ye images and icons,
O ye analogies and symbols that speak of God,
Bless ye the Lord; praise him and magnify him for ever.

You are 'the fullness of God' with love 'beyond knowledge';
'High and lifted up' and in the depths of the soul.
You encompass and surround us as you work your will among us.
Dwell within us and around us, above us and beneath us;
Let us grasp 'what is the breadth and length and height and depth' of your love.
Let the fullness of yourself strengthen our inner being and all that we are with the power of your Spirit.
Let the language barriers be broken.

Mature Manhood

Ephesians 4.7-8, 11-16

Mature.
Come of age.
Grown up into Christ.
High calling indeed.
For the full stature of Christ is the stature of service.
The body is to be built up in love.

Here is a vision of the church,
Interdependent and one,
Making its members into men.
For the true humanity is Christ.

Here is a vision of mankind,
Interdependent and one,
Building itself up in love.
For the Christian *is* man and man is of Christ.

Lord, you are the God made man, who has made man part of your life and part of yourself.
You are the God made man, who inspires us to attain to that maturity of manhood which is yourself.
Draw us with our gifts, with our talents, with our individuality,
Draw us into your body, the body of mankind, and make us free.

'Devices of the Devil'

Ephesians 6.10-18; Romans 13.12-14

For her it was the feeling that nothing would go right,
That all her attempts to succeed would come to nought,
That whatever she did was doomed from the start.
It felt as if the world was against her.
She seemed ensnared by forces that she did not understand,
And turned in on herself with a cry of despair.
The powers of darkness prevailed.

For me it is the feeling that I have been here before,
That I am tasting the failure of sin yet again.
I seek to refrain but it does not do much good.
The forces that hold me in their grip seem too strong.
They lodge within and find an accomplice.
The 'armour of God' lies forgotten or is laid aside,
And the powers of darkness prevail.

Lord of power,
Lord of strength,
You stand supreme against all that opposes your will.
Stand with us 'when things are at their worst'.

Giving Thanks in Prison

Philippians 1

In prison for his faith,
But more concerned for the church's witness than for himself,
Forging in his experience his theology of the church,
Gaining encouragement from his understanding of the Body of Christ.
'Incorporate in Christ Jesus ... you all share in the privilege that is mine.'
Here is confidence, Lord,
Confidence that you were with him through the prayers of the church,
That they were 'contending as one man for the gospel faith'.
In times of stress or isolation,
When visible links are broken,
And a man stands on his own,
It is a great thing to know that one small unit in the life of the church gains its vitality from the whole.
It is a great thing to know that the strength of the Spirit reaches out into the most isolated limb of the Body.
It is a great thing to look outwards and give thanks.

Humility

Philippians 2.1-13; 1 Peter 5.5b-7

Hope for humility is itself humbled if man is all.
For then he is left to work out his salvation alone.
There can indeed be care and sacrifice and a displeasing of self,
But it always seems provisional with the sights set low.
Once you convince us, Lord, that man is not alone,
You raise humility to the heavens by descending yourself to the depths,
And placing the power and the glory in the abandonment of privilege and pride.
You give us a focus beyond ourselves.
You work within us as we work ourselves.
You release the human potential that is there as you lower our need for equality with God.
Be with me, Lord,
Turning my will into yours.

'So Much Garbage'

Philippians 3

He had everything going for him.
Irreproachable testimony to his Jewishness.
Impeccable credentials.
And all he cared for was his knowledge of Christ.
In one sense, Lord, it's incredible to have all this and yet to count it as nought.
A lesser man might do this as inverted snobbery.
He could afford to discount the value of the qualifications he has, when everyone knows that he has them.
For then he gains all round.
Those who respect the marks of his status know that he has them and build him up large.
While those who respect even more his show of humility can build him up larger still.
But Paul was beyond all this,
'Forgetting what is behind him, and reaching out for that which lies ahead.'
Lord, 'transfigure this body that belongs to our humble state,
Give it a form like that of your own resplendent body.'
Subject me to yourself.

Too Near for Comfort

Philippians 4.6-7

He is a loner by temperament;
He holds himself back from relationships,
Withdrawn and shy;
Needing friendship yet afraid of its demands;
Anxious when others get too close,
So anxious that the defensive barriers remain.
In large measure he has rationalized his anxiety by deepening his clear competence and capability in areas where people only slightly impinge upon him;
And where they do touch his world he has the techniques developed for holding them at arm's length.
This way his anxiety is turned to advantage and his withdrawnness boosts his confidence in his capacity to cope.
It is not surprising that his relationship with you, Lord, runs along the same lines.
He prays, he says, but can't stand you being too close.
His prayers are formal and fixed and come to an end if he senses that you might be too near.
It all has to be firmly structured if he is to preserve a modicum of peace,
But it is a shallow peace.

Work within, Lord,
Slowly, gradually coming nearer with a deeper peace,
A peace as yet 'beyond his utmost understanding'.

The Body of Christ at Work

Philippians 4.10-20; 2 Corinthians 8.1-15

Practical theology,
The Body of Christ at work.
The burden of his troubles shared.
His financial needs supplied.
But he still had his pride.
'Do not think that I set my heart upon the gift.'
'I have learned to find resources in myself whatever my circumstances.'
It is not an easy thing to accept the help on which one is dependent.
It is not an easy thing however much a man believes in the interdependence of the Body.
And yet it is the very heart of the gospel that 'your surplus meets their need, but one day your need may be met from their surplus',
The point where theology touches earth and takes on its meaning.
Lord, give us strength to share,
And the strength to receive.

Key to the Cosmos

Colossians 1.13-20, 2.9-15; Ephesians 1.7-10

Lord of forgiveness, Lord of freedom,
You are encountered in experience,
You bring light into 'the domain of darkness',
You stand sovereign above the emotions and the mind and the imagination of man.
But there has to be more if this sovereignty is to remain secure.
A lord of experience alone is a fickle lord who comes and goes, dependent on feelings, a projection in the mind.
It has to be that you who are encountered in experience are the Lord of creation,
Sustaining the world in which you are found.
In Christ you are the point of it all,
The meaning of the universe,
The key to the cosmos.
You reveal the pattern of all things,
That love and forgiveness and grace are at the heart of it all,
Inviting us to bring your creation to its fulfilment in you.

Baptismal Burial

Colossians 2.12, 3.1-17; Philippians 1.21; Romans 6.3-11

The turning point has been reached.
The crucial decision made.
They had died to their former life.
They had been buried with Christ in their baptism,
And been raised into newness of life.
Physical death has lost its sting,
For 'life is Christ and death gain'.

There is a new meaning to life, Lord, for the man who lives in you.
There is a new dimension to all that he is and all that he does.
There is a depth within him that enables him to face all the worst that life can throw at him and emerge giving thanks.
But the failures are still real.
The bonds that bind us to the old nature are stronger than we care to admit.
But they no longer have the final say, for the bonds are there to be cut.
Let our life be your life, Lord.
Make us yours.

'Like a Thief in the Night'

1 Thessalonians 5.1-11

The Day of the Lord is a day of judgment and joy that 'comes like a thief in the night'.
It is a day as sudden in its coming as 'the pangs that come upon a woman with child'.
The advent of God brings light to the world and reveals the darkness for what it is.
It puts life in perspective and sets the tone.
But darkness and light, judgment and joy are with us now.
You have seen to that, Lord, and turned the time of the End into a minor matter.
You judge and bring joy.
You sustain and challenge.
And you do it now.
Your advent once is an advent for all time.
Your Day is now, your Day is always.
Be the consummation of all things in yourself.
Bring all 'to the full attainment of salvation'.
And keep us to the end in company with yourself.

Inspiration

1 Thessalonians 5.19-23; Galatians 5.22

He believes he is inspired.
He speaks his mind.
He speaks as a prophet.
He speaks strongly and well.
He speaks for all the world to hear.
He speaks and inspires with a message that divides.
He speaks – or does he? Is it your voice within, Lord?
We like to claim that our words are your words, our thoughts your thoughts.
But are you so easily dragged in as the source of all the deepest convictions in any man's life?
We speak and preach and invoke your name.
We speak and preach and say contradictory things.
There is no danger of 'stifling inspiration'.
Rather there is need to 'bring it to the test', to separate the fruit from the weeds.
For the 'fruit of the Spirit' is the test of inspiration.
The fruit of the Spirit is the test of ourselves.

Make us 'holy in every part'.
Keep us 'sound in spirit'.

Specious Speculation

1 Timothy 1.3-4; Titus 3.9; Genesis 2.16-17, 3.1-5

Mythological mathematics.
Specious speculations.
Astrological assaults on the stars.
But there is more to it than this.
They are all attempts to predict the plan of the Lord,
 to catch and control the mind of Christ.
We like to know, Lord, to know as we are known, to have the facts at our fingertips.
Faith is all very well, but faith is second best.
We want to know because knowledge brings control.
We want to know because knowledge gives us our 'place' in the scheme of things.
We want to know because the fruit of the tree of knowledge will make us as the gods, and if we are as gods we can work on our own.
We want to know.
But you 'work through faith' so that we can work together.
This is the way it goes.
Let us reconcile ourselves to it, Lord, but it is not all that easy.
Let us live in faith.
Let us rely on you.
Let us work together.

First Things First

1 Timothy 2.1-7

'*First of all* I urge that prayers be offered for all men, for the sovereign and all in high office . . .'
Order within society must be part of your will, Lord,
For your world is to be one and your people are to be one.
For this Christ died.
First of all our concern is to be with 'the nations'.
For there is one God 'whose will it is that all men . . . should come to know the truth'.

Let your church, us, me get our priorities straight, Lord.
'In the beginning' the world was your initial concern.

The Demands of Leadership

1 Timothy 3.1-13; Titus 1.5-9

I suppose it is inevitable, but it seems rather hard.
It seems rather hard that any man who leads has to live with greater demands being made on his personal life than would be expected of another.
He must be 'a man of unimpeachable character', but where is there such a man?
Forgiveness is so tightly controlled that it is only allowed to reach out to him in a modest and small measure.
It seems rather hard, but I suppose it is inevitable.
For the man who leads represents what he leads.
A failure of his is so easily generalized as a failure of the whole.
But surely with the church, Lord, the whole is strong enough to carry failure, for the whole includes you.

Forgive leaders who fail, for otherwise how can I ever be forgiven?
And give me strength to bear the demands of leadership in areas where oversight is mine.

Widows on the Roll

1 Timothy 5.3-16

It is a bit pompous, Lord.
True, there is love working itself out in deed.
An example being set of congregational care.
Support being given where support is needed.
But it still smacks of the pomposity of rules.
The widow 'must produce evidence of good deeds performed'.
Has she cared for children?
Has she given hospitality?
Has she washed the feet of God's people?
Has she supported those in distress?
An eye for an eye, and a tooth for a tooth.
In so far as you have done it unto them, you have done it for yourself.
Your good deeds get you on the roll.
Her good deeds are a sign of her faith, but does she have to justify herself?
For any man or woman of the Spirit knows that his or her own good deeds always fall short of what they might have been.
Is she forced to justify herself?
See, how good I have been!
Aren't there others who can speak for her?
Let us take care, Lord, in forcing people to justify themselves.
For their only justification is that which you alone can give them.

'Healing for all Mankind'

Titus 2.11-15

Wholeness and healing.
What is your model of man?
To heal is to change, to alter for good.
It is positive and holy and strives to remake.
But what is to be remade?
What is your model of man?
A leg is broken and made whole again.
When cells are destroyed we have a war on our hands.
Our model is the body functioning and free.
But with matters of mind and morals the story is different.
When a man is depressed we seek to lift the gloom.
But if he is manic and high we seek to dampen him down.
One man is condemned by guilt feelings within.
Another knows no guilt and we think it all wrong.
One man is moral and rules with a rod.
Another is permissive and his limits are few.
Wholeness and healing.
What is your model of man?

My model is a man who lives for the world.
My model is a man orientated to God.
My model is a man who challenges to decision.
My model is a man whose concern is men.
My model is a man who suffers and dies.
My model is Christ who heals by love.
My model is Christ who brings man to the wholeness of God.
My model is Christ in whom, Lord, let us live.

A Personal Touch

Philemon

A personal touch.
Onesimus has fallen on his feet.
How could Philemon refuse to have him back – 'more than a slave, a dear brother, very dear indeed to me, and how much dearer to you?'
Paul was pulling all the strings, playing on a man's sense of indebtedness and love, with the possibility (or was it a threat?) of a visit thrown in.
The letter is a command for all its tactful note of appeal.
And why not?
Why not use all the influence one can to gain freedom even for one man?

A Word to Jews

It would be surprising if a letter to Jews was not predominantly Jewish in outlook. Its central theme is priesthood and many of its presuppositions belong to the world of the Old Testament. This fact perhaps puts this letter second only to the Revelation of John in the hierarchy of difficulty for the contemporary Christian. If, however, we are persuaded that the God who 'has spoken to us in this final age in the Son whom he has made heir to the whole universe' also 'spoke to our forefathers in former times' if only 'in fragmentary and varied fashion' (Hebrews 1.1-2), then this may encourage us to open the letter in an attempt to let its message speak to us.

The Breaking of Death

Hebrews 2.9, 14-18

Hope in the test of suffering.
Liberation from fear.
The breaking of death.
You are one with us, Lord.
You share the same flesh and blood.
You taste torment and suffering.
You face anxiety and fear as you pass through death into life.
Death is broken.
Man is free.

It is easy to say it.
The word of encouragement.
The boost to confidence.
The slap in the face for the one who 'has death at his command'.
But there are many who have 'all their lifetime been in servitude',
Chained and fettered in a personality that smells of death.
Many who long for liberation and the subjection of fear,
But somehow are never able to hold on to you as you pass through their suffering.

And what of me?
Sometimes we walk together in triumph through the anxieties and tests of life.
Sometimes I leave it to you, Lord, the suffering part, and stand by as a spectator.
Sometimes we set out together, but courage fails in the heat of it all; the way forward is frightening, the way back is blocked.
Stand with me, Lord, and let me know your presence.

Cutting Words

Hebrews 4.12-13

Her words too were 'active and alive'.
They 'cut more keenly than any two-edged sword'.
They cut to hurt, piercing to the heart.
They were words of bitterness, soaked in sarcasm.
They were the words of a woman with more hate than happiness in her heart.

There are many kinds of active, cutting words, Lord, words alive with power.
The difference between them is the difference of those who deliver them.
For words are an extension of the person who speaks them.
Your word is yourself, alive with love,
As sharp as a knife that excises malignant growth.
Your word is yourself and you urge us to be full of it.
Your word is yourself and you urge us to speak it.
Your word is yourself and you share it with us.

The High Priest Put in his Place

Hebrews 3.1, 4.14-5.10, 7.1-3, 10.11-25

The ritual of running repairs to the covenant is his job.
Repetitious ritual for renewing a relationship with God.
The machinery of men for closing the breach.
A man to offer sacrifice for sin.
A holy man to enter the Holy of Holies to form that fragile link with the forgiveness of God.
The ritual is emptied of meaning.
The High Priest has been put in his place.

For the High Priest is Christ, the 'priest for ever', who 'has passed through the heavens' as the way to the Father,
The way to newness of life,
The life of which you are the source,
The life that no longer depends on a man's scrupulous care to dispose of his sin.
The procedural path to the graciousness of your love is seen for what it is, a path paved with good intentions and totally irrelevant to our needs,
A path trodden, trodden, and trodden again.
A sacrifice here and a sacrifice there, with a man set apart to negotiate the deal.
You have cut through all this, Lord.
You have shared our humanity to show us that you wish us to share your life.
'Let us draw near with a true heart, in full assurance of faith.'

The Priest who Sacrificed Himself

Hebrews 9.11-15, 10.1-10

The great concern.
Not only was he the High Priest, the status-man, triumphantly mediating the message.
The means of the mediation was the death of himself.
There was no other way to show the extent to which his love would go.
'The blood of his sacrifice was his own blood.'
No substitute sacrifice, no ersatz death.
We can spare a goat or two, a few prayers, loose change for the collection, the odds and ends that seem important until we are confronted with the real thing in offerings.
The shadow has hardened into the true image.

Lord, remake us in that image,
The image of yourself.
Put substance into our sharing your body and your blood.

The Nebulous Realities

Hebrews 11.1-12.2

The nebulous realities.
The intangible hopes that mould a man's actions.
The hidden values that fashion his life but can never be proved.
'By faith we perceive that the universe was fashioned by the word of God so that the visible came forth from the invisible.'
History is full of men who knew that there was more to life than the tangible world around them;
Men who have staked everything on a vision, a dream, an ideal that made them almost 'too good for this world'.

'And what of ourselves, with all these witnesses to faith around us?'
Give us courage, Lord, confidence in yourself, amidst the pressures that prise us away from the values that are at the core of the universe.
Keep our eyes fixed firmly on you, who endured the ultimate in pain to remain true to the ultimate meaning of life.

‘Remember Where you Stand’

Hebrews 12.18-29

‘Remember where you stand.’
That extra dimension to life.

I stand before my fine house, detached and private, with my polished car gleaming in the sun, the city of my living self, unshakeable and strong.
I stand in ‘darkness and gloom’, in the desert of Sinai, before a tyrant god who fills me with fear.
I stand before a man who despises the colour of my face and studiously ignores my request for attention.
I stand before my wife in joy and hope of the love that is about to be shared.
I stand out from my friends as a failure and a bore who embarrasses them all by my presence.
I stand out from the mass by virtue of my job which gives me all the status and fame that I need.

‘Remember where you stand.’
That extra dimension to life.
For you stand before the presence of God,
Before ‘the city of the living God’ within the kingdom that is unshakeable should the foundation of the heavens and earth collapse.
Lord, let me ‘hear the voice that speaks’.
‘Let me give thanks and worship.’

A Few Words to the World

We now turn to the seven short letters ascribed to James, Peter, John and Jude (the 'catholic' letters, so-called presumably because of their general appeal to the church at large in comparison with the Pauline correspondence to specific churches or people). Discussion continues concerning their connection with the people whose names they bear. If they do not have apostolic authorship, then they belong to the end of the first century AD or the early part of the second. Here, as with the Pauline letters, our concern is with their contents.

The World v. God

James 4.1-4; 1 John 2.15-17, 5.4b-5; John 3.16

It depends on the point of viewing, for the world is ambiguous and points both ways.
'Anyone who loves the world is a stranger to the Father's love,'
For 'love of the world is enmity to God'.
So turn from the world and live in Christ.
There is more to this than a right-wing reaction against 'all that panders to the appetites, or entices the eyes, all the glamour of its life'.
For the world is a world of suffering and evil and often seems thoroughly 'godless'.
In moments of desperation or despair, Lord, when things look black, a man can easily see victory in your power to bring it all to an end.

And yet the world is your world, the object of your love.
'For God so loved the world that he sent his Son.'
The world is the place of meeting between man and yourself.
So seek Christ in and through the world.
There is more to this than a left-wing sense of liberation and permissive freedom.
For the world is a world of value and joy and goodness which mirrors your love.
Here a man sees victory in your power to bring the world to its fulfilment in you.

Lord, continue to love your world.
Let us love it enough to co-operate with your will for the world.

Healing and Wholeness

James 5.13-18

I have two problems about it, Lord.
The first is this:
Many a man has prayed for health, believing in your power, but has had to be satisfied with a success somewhat less than that of Elijah,
And then perhaps has despaired of his faith, or of your love.
Sometimes, of course, we add the semi-sophisticated insertion – 'if it be your will'.
Do we attempt to have the cake and eat it?
Your power is preserved should there be no cure, but deep down secretly we pray to make it your will, to change your will indeed.
And here is a second problem:
If it is your will, here and there in answer to a prayer, to alter a man's situation with a cure, then why don't you pull out the stops for the sake of all who suffer?
And yet still I pray:
Heal, Lord, heal.
Encourage us to use all our resources to heal.
And help us too to see your healing work in the widest terms.
Bring wholeness, salvation, reconciliation with yourself, especially where there is no cure.
Deepen our faith in you as the Lord who suffers along with the sufferer.
This is a 'powerful and effective' result of prayer.

The Calling of a Christian

1 Peter 2.9, 4.12-16; Exodus 19.5-6; Isaiah 43.20-21

Words culled from the Old Testament.
Words with a wealth of associations behind them.
'Chosen race.'
'Royal priesthood.'
'Dedicated nation.'
'People claimed by God for his own.'
But it is the new associations that matter now.
To be chosen is a privilege, but now the implications are made known.
To be royal and priestly is an honour, but now the nature of the sacrifice is seen.
To be dedicated is a source for pride, but now the dedication is declared to be 'even unto death'.
To be claimed by God is redemption, but now the nature of the claimant is known.

Lord, I am identified with the body to whom all this applies.
Help us, help me to be identified with all that this implies.

To Heap or Not to Heap?

1 Peter 3.8-15, 4.7-11

'Be one in thought and feeling.'
It is easier said than done, Lord.
I am sure it is right.
To heap abuse on abuse;
To retaliate when attacked;
To come out fighting and furious;
All this is natural but simply serves to add to the number of already 'innumerable sins'.
We soon learn the weapons that wound, the particular words that cut to hurt.
Our arsenal is stocked and guarded.
And we think it a source of pride if we can mature enough only to draw our weapons in self-defence.

To heap love on abuse;
To retaliate with blessing;
To come out welcoming and free;
All these are signs of the strength that you supply which slowly serves to cancel those 'innumerable sins'.
Lord, let us 'love life and see good days'.
Let us 'seek peace and pursue it'.
Let us empty our arsenals.
Let the source of our pride be that your glory shines through our lives.

The Vitality of God

2 Peter 1.16-19; 1 Peter 1.3-7

Some vision in life,
Some direction,
Something like a 'shining lamp' that gives meaning to it all;
This is the desire.
We yearn for it, if we do not have it.
We are sometimes assailed by doubts when we do have it.
'Tales artfully spun' catch the imagination for a time, but something which lasts is the only thing that satisfies.

You, Lord, are the direction, the purpose, the meaning of it all.
You are the vitality of God for his 'favour rests upon you'.
You are the vitality of God giving 'new birth into a living hope ... that nothing can destroy'.
We have heard it and seen it in moments on the 'mountain'.
Come, Lord Jesus.
Revitalize our lives.

The Lie

1 John 2.3-6, 3.16-18, 4.20-21; James 1.22-27, 2.14-20

'If a man does not love the brother whom he has seen, it cannot be that he loves God whom he has not seen.'

And yet it can seem much easier to fall in love with a god who keeps well out of the way and remains unseen, than with the brother who is often far too visible for comfort, the anxiety-provoking brother whom I wish I had not seen, the infuriating brother whom fate seems to have wished upon me.

This is the crux of faith, to love the brother whom I wish I did not have to love, but who is the locus of your presence.

James and John are shouting it out loud, Lord.

It is easy enough to say it.

It is easy enough even to believe it;

That faith and good deeds are two sides of the same coin;

That faith only becomes faith in you when it is a response to you in others;

That we tell a lie if we profess a faith that is denied by our lives.

It is easy enough to say it and believe it.

We have heard it all before.

A suitable passage for slipping into a service with a built-in sermon that gives a boost to our guilt and maybe also to our offering for Christian Aid.

But the easiest thing of all is to live the lie and to deny it to ourselves.

For the lie is life, the life we lead.

The lie is life, for any man's life is always less than it might be.

The lie is life until the time comes when you will be all in all.

Let us not simply live with the lie, Lord, but see through it.

And strengthen us to let you in.

Strengthen us to let you work within us and through us to lay down that life for the sake of others.

Perfection is a Pipe-Dream, but Some Love is There

1 John 4.16b-19

'Perfect love banishes fear!'
Perfection is a long way off.
She feels that she is not loved, not accepted.
She feels that he always puts her second, behind his work, his activities, his friends.
She fears that her marriage is near the rocks.

He feels that her demands are excessive.
He feels that she is constantly getting at him, undermining all he does.
He too is afraid that he can stand it no longer, that his anger must out, that the marriage is tearing apart.

'Fear brings with it the pains of judgment, and anyone who is afraid has not attained to love in its perfection.'
They blame each other, and both feel judged.
Perfection is a pipe-dream for them, but some love is still there.
Can they build on this?
Can they break out of the vicious circle of mutual reproach?
Can either of them hold back the condemnation and waive the right of defence?
Can either of them remove the sting of the other's reproach at the moment of attack?
Help them, Lord.
Help them to help themselves.
Help me to help them to help themselves.
Dwell in them, for you are love.

Purveyors of Porn

Jude

'Remember Sodom and Gomorrah.'
He whets the appetites with his hints.
What on earth were they doing?
'Licentiousness ... unnatural lusts ... defiling the body ... brute beasts ... a blot on the love-feasts.'
The voyeurs are vying for the view.
But they get the full treatment from this defender of the faith.
They presumably posed a real threat to the church.
'You, my friends, must fortify yourselves in your most sacred faith ... and snatch doubting souls from the flames.'
Modern man, I suppose, might smile in sophistication and speak of an inhibited sexuality lurking beneath this tirade.
And he may be right. Who knows?
But what matters to Jude most is 'the love of God' to whom 'be glory and majesty, might and authority, through Jesus Christ our Lord'.

The Last Word from Patmos

The Revelation of John is an account of visionary experiences of 'what must shortly happen', though it is difficult to be certain about the nature of this expected event. The most likely explanation is that it is not simply a description of the historical run-up to the end of the world, but that John has made use of the current symbolic language of the End to describe the imminent ordeal of persecution and suffering that many in the church were going to have to face. Thus, however powerful and threatening the signs of evil confronting the Christian, they would be broken before the power of God.

This book, written about the end of the first century AD, clearly belongs to a cultural background we no longer share. Its first readers would presumably be fluent in the symbolic language and imagery of the visions in a way that we are not, however sympathetic our interest. And yet in spite of this the writer's strong faith in the sovereignty of his Lord comes through these bizarre apocalyptic visions. The End to which he points is a person – the First and the Last, the Alpha and Omega – whose presence encounters man in the midst of time. No matter what ordeal man must face, no matter 'what must shortly happen', no matter what cataclysmic events there are in a man's experience, the reader is encouraged to remain confident that they are the locus of Christ's presence and that through them God is working out his purpose.

Faith at First Hand

Revelation 1.4-20

'Write down what you have seen,'
The things you know from experience to be true,
And only the things you know.
Faith at first hand.
For John it was visions,
Esoteric visions that some have turned into a playground for dating the End,
Whilc many of us find them the most difficult of writings to read.
And yet visions of the First and the Last, the Alpha and Omega, the Beginning and the End, the living one who was dead but is alive for evermore, the one who is strength when all else is at an end.
'Write down what you have seen,'
And only what you have seen.

I have seen no visions, Lord,
Only a glimpse of you as the 'sovereign Lord of all'.

Seven Churches under Review

Revelation 2.1-3.22

Pro and con,
For and against,
The churches under review.
Are they in a fit state for a confrontation with crisis?
How many of them will be victorious?
Men and women have to stand up and be counted,
Their faith buffeted by persecution and suffering.
Are the foundations of rock or of sand?

The question turns us back on ourselves.
Faith is often weak,
'Neither hot nor cold'.
Sometimes it's strong—at least stronger, strengthened, or so it feels.
But the test, the ordeal, the suffering, the crisis of persecution belong to other lands.
Here critical moments have a different shape.
Let us face these with strength.
Let us be 'faithful till death'.
'And do not bring us to the test.'

Praise

Revelation 4, 7.9-17, 21.1-7

It was a tremendous experience.
A glorious outburst of praise.
Emotions given full freedom.
Depths of feeling soaring from within.
Individuals bonded together reaching out beyond themselves.
'Praise and glory and wisdom, thanksgiving and honour, power and might be to our God for ever and ever.'
The intensity of the experience surprised me.
It was only an ordinary service, though the church was packed for the festival.
It was only an ordinary service but with a touch of eternity about it.
'Then I saw a new heaven and a new earth, for the first heaven and the first earth had vanished ... Now at last God has his dwelling among men!'
There is no denying the transforming nature of the experience.
You were there with us, Lord, giving us a taste of eternity, giving us strength in our self-expression to be with you in the earthiness of life.
Be with us here, where the 'first earth' is not yet renewed.
Be with us as the focus of our praise.

A Bride for the Lamb

Revelation 19.6-9, 22.16-17, 20; 2 Corinthians 11.2; Ephesians 4.23-24

The wedding of the Lamb.
Without us it cannot go on,
For we are not only invited, we are the bride betrothed to Christ.
'Come, Lord Jesus.'
Work within your church.
Let it be made ready to be robed in 'the righteous deeds of God's people',
Clothed in 'the new nature that is of God's creating'.
'Come, Lord Jesus.'
For left to ourselves we would remain unmarried for ever.
Here we stand
In the midst of this world, in the ordinariness of life, in the routine of living;
Here we stand
Firm perhaps in the desire, but more fickle in our readiness.
Come among us, Lord.
Strengthen us.
Direct your church to become what it might be, and indeed ultimately is, in your scheme of things.
'Come, Lord Jesus.'

Appendix: A Brief Bibliography

Commentaries

A. E. Harvey, *Companion to the New Testament*, OUP and CUP 1970. A splendid commentary for use alongside the New English Bible text. A large book but the one to have if only one commentary is to be used.

J. L. Houlden, *Paul's Letters from Prison*, Penguin Books 1970. In the series of the Pelican New Testament Commentaries, and dealing with Philippians, Colossians, Philemon and Ephesians.

The series of *Torch Bible Commentaries*, published by SCM Press, covers all the writings from the Acts to Revelation.

General Books

T. G. A. Baker, *What is The New Testament?*, SCM Press 1969. An excellent book which, *inter alia*, has a chapter on Paul and also raises interesting questions concerning the unity and diversity of the New Testament, its authority, and how to understand and interpret it.

A. M. Hunter, *Introducing the New Testament*, SCM Press 1972. A chapter on each of the New Testament books 'to mediate the findings of scholars in a simple untechnical form'.

The Gospel According to St Paul, SCM Press 1966. A useful little book on the way Paul saw it.

Index of Passages

Old Testament Passages

Gospel Passages